THAI COUNTRY COOKING

FROM

LAGUNA BEACH RESORT

Laguna Beach Resort

LAGUNA PHUKET

THAI COUNTRY COOKING

I would like to thank everyone involved in making this project a reality. Of course, Chef Theerati, Chef Yuthinan and their teams, who put the recipes and menus together. Then, Executive Chef Rainer Roersch and Simon Dornan, who tirelessly checked all the recipes and made sure the photography went according to plan, Grenville Fordham for the design and editing, David Found for the photography and, last but not least, James Sullivan-Tailyour who oversaw the whole project from start to finish.

Jörg A. Hauri
General Manager

Laguna Beach Resort
Bangtao Bay, Phuket 83110,Thailand
Tel : 66 7632 4352   Fax : 66 7632 4353
e-mail : info@lagunabeach-resort.com
website : www.lagunabeach-resort.com

Published by Laguna Beach Resort 2002

ISBN 974-90157-4-6

Editorial & design by
IMAGE asia
10/3 Moo 2 Chalong,
Muang, Phuket 83000, Thailand
Tel : 66 7628 2198-9
Fax : 66 7628 2198
email : info@image-asia.com

Photography by
IMAGE asia / David Found

Colour separation & printing by
Limmark Advertising, Phuket, Thailand

CONTENTS

AN INTRODUCTION

TO THAI COUNTRY COOKING

Thailand has one of the most varied cuisines in the world. It encompasses the whole range of tastes from fiery-hot to mild, sweet to sour, rich to simple – and everything in between. There are regional variations as well as the differences between 'high' and 'low' cooking. The former is epitomised by Royal Thai Cuisine, once served only in the Royal Household, while a sample of the latter could be the simple, *Som Tam*, a northeastern regional dish made from unripe papaya, and a firm national favourite throughout society.

There is a world of difference between the dishes you might find on the menu in most first-class Thai restaurants – including those overseas – and what Thai people normally cook at home.

The idea behind 'Thai Country Cooking' is to bring you closer to the real Thailand. To give you the chance to cook at home for your friends and family, whether for a lunchtime snack or an important celebration, the kind of food Thais themselves would cook for similar occasions.

To guide you through your first attemps, our recipes are supplemented by four set menu suggestions – where you can take advantage of our chefs' experience in what make the best combinations. Finally, the feature stories and the introductions to sections provide an insight into what Thai food is about, its main characteristics and some of the history behind its development.

ABBREVIATIONS USED IN RECIPES

gm = gramme(s) ; 1 oz = 28 gm approx
tsp = teaspoon; tbsp = tablespoon; pch = pinch

SERVINGS

Thai food is presented as a number of different, shared dishes. Each recipe is sufficient for one 'dish', which – alone – would normally serve one person. If catering for 4 people, we recommend you prepare 4 dishes.

A HISTORY

OF THAI FOOD

The culture of Thailand is rich and varied, and its food a magnificent reflection of this diversity.

Thailand's location in the middle of Southeast Asia has made it a crossroads and a destination for a wide array of cultural and ethnic groups. Each group, whether transitory or permanent, has left its imprint on the country's cuisine.

The classic example of influence from a transitory group is the chili. Native to the Americas, it was brought to Thailand about 400 years ago by Portuguese traders. The Thais, who had previously used copious quantities of black peppercorns to provide spicy heat to their cooking, welcomed the chili with open arms into their cuisine.

ORIGINALLY NATIVE TO THE AMERICAS, THE CHILI WAS FIRST BROUGHT TO THAILAND ABOUT 400 YEARS AGO BY PORTUGUESE TRADERS

Groups that have migrated to Thailand and taken up residence have had a less incendiary, but even broader, impact on Thai culinary habits. It would, for example, be impossible to talk about Thai food without looking at the enormous contributions made by Chinese immigrants. Two salient examples are the *wok* found in every Thai kitchen and the noodles eaten almost every day of the year by practically every single Thai.

It must never be forgotten, however, that none of this has taken place in a vacuum. These culinary implants have interacted with each other and with the culture present in the country when they arrived. This means that Thailand's cuisine is not part *this* and part *that*. It is a blend that is unique and distinctly Thai – and something that can be found nowhere else in the world.

There is yet another factor that has played a significant role in the development of Thailand's cuisine, one that is only partially cultural: Thailand has an enormous amount of geographical diversity for such a small country, and this has caused cooking styles and tastes to develop that reflect the regional differences in climate, soil and preferences.

NORTH
Chiangmai
NORTHEAST
CENTRAL
Bangkok
SOUTH
Phuket

REGIONAL
VARIATIONS

THE NORTH

Sandwiched between Myanmar (formerly Burma) and Laos, northern Thailand is filled with mountains – the foothills of the Himalayas. Burmese and Laotian influences are obvious in the local food. Northerners are fond of the "sticky rice" popular in Laos. They'll sit on the floor around a *khan toke,* a small low table made of teak or lacquer, and dunk sticky rice and fresh vegetables into a dipping sauce. Several sauces are used, *naam prik ohng* the most popular. Made from chili paste, fried pork and chopped tomatoes, it is reminiscent of spaghetti sauce. Northern food is usually very simple. *Ook gai,* a rustic chicken curry is typical. Made with lots of lemongrass and wild citrus leaves, but no coconut, it is always eaten with sticky rice, eagerly dipped into the citrus flavoured sauce.

THE NORTHEAST

This region, known as *Isarn,* encompasses approximately one-third of Thailand. Separated from Laos by the Mekong River and from Cambodia and the fertile Chao Phrya River Basin by mountains, it is a rocky plateau with soil that hasn't been nurtured by floodwaters. The weather is hot, and the rains erratic, but torrential when they do come. These factors conspire to make farming and life for the people of the area difficult.

The cuisine that has developed is one of the most popular regional cuisines in Thailand, and it is difficult to go anywhere in the Kingdom without finding a restaurant serving *Isarn* food. The food is characterized by grilled meats, fiery sauces, and sticky rice. In addition, a salad called *som tam,* made with sour shredded green papaya and a combination of sweet, salty and spicy ingredients, is one of Thailand's most popular dishes.

CENTRAL THAILAND

Central Thailand at one time lay beneath the sea, but over the years the silt in rivers descending from the Himalayas filled the area with rich soil. Today it is Thailand's breadbasket: a vast, fertile inland delta crammed with farms and rice paddies. The cooks of this area have much to work with and have developed what most people equate with 'Thai food'. Dishes from this region fall into two basic categories: Palace cooking, the elegant and elaborate food associated with royalty, and home cooking, the stuff ordinary folks eat. Palace-style cooking is elaborate and

THE NORTH

THE NORTHEAST

CENTRAL

THE SOUTH

time consuming. Presentation is as important as taste, so a lot of time is spent carving fruits and vegetables into intricate shapes. The curries contain rich sweet sauces made from coconut milk, what people abroad generally identify as Thai food. *Gaeng khiaow waan gai,* or green chicken curry, is one of these dishes, but visitors are often surprised at how much hotter it is in Thailand than at home. Royalty may prefer sweet coconut curries, but as with all Thais, they like them spicy.

Home cooking in the central region is not as complex, but no less delicious. One dish that is representative and popular with both visitors and Thais alike is *phad grapaow.* In this dish minced pork, beef or chicken is sautéed with garlic, chilies, and *grapao* (sometimes called holy basil) and then poured over rice. The result is simple, unique, delicious and memorable.

The South

Southern Thailand is situated on the long, narrow Malaysian Peninsula. This means that seafood is an important item in the region's food, and that the area is relatively isolated from much of the rest of the country. It also means that the cultural influences have been different.

Many in the south are M uslim, who don't eat pork. There are also subtle influences from India, particularly in the spices that are used. Turmeric, for example, is found in many dishes served in the south.

Southern Thais like their food hot and sour, reflected in many of their favourite curries and soups. They also like bitter tastes, making the *sataw* bean very popular. This bean, that grows in gigantic pods, is found in markets throughout southern Thailand (but is difficult to find elsewhere). Shrimp sautéed with *sataw* beans, or *goong phad sataw,* is a simple stir-fried dish of shrimps, *sataw* beans, garlic, fish sauce and sugar. Although pungent and bitter, some visitors find it an interesting change of pace.

Coastal Areas

Thailand has a long coastline for a country its size, and though it hosts a wide variety of cultural groups, there are enough similarities in the food to treat it as a single culinary region.

Seafood, served in a wide variety of ways, is the star of the show: barbecued, steamed, stir-fried, raw, cooked in liquids and grilled in foil or banana leaf envelopes. Thailand's seafood dishes are among the country's least complex, but a sauce is usually served to "dress it up" , either as a part of the dish or served on the side.

There is nothing more delicious than a delicate steamed fish, an art in which Thais excel. It comes to the table moist, full of flavour and easy to eat. *Pla neung manao* is especially good. Here garlic, chilies and lime juice are spread on a fish before steaming. When served, the garlic and chilies are pushed aside, leaving the fish resting in a delicious lemony sauce.

Spices, Herbs

& Other Ingredients

The food of Thailand acquires its unique aroma and taste from a relatively small number of ingredients.

Most of these items are used by other cuisines, but the Thais often employ them in larger amounts or in combinations rarely seen elsewhere, resulting in a cuisine that is distinct and readily identifiable.

In recent years, the popularity of Thai food has made most of these ingredients available in large cities throughout the world.

CHILIES give Thai food the hallmark spiciness of the cuisine. The tiny *prik kee noo suan* is the hottest and most popular. *Prik kee noo* are slightly larger and marginally less hot. *Prik chee fah* resemble the jalapeno, often used in Latin America and have a comparable amount of heat. The pale green *prik chee fah* are larger and usually less incendiary.

FISH SAUCE, made from fermented anchovies, is used extensively in Thailand. It provides salt and is a valuable source of protein and minerals.

COCONUT MILK AND CREAM, usually made from fresh coconuts in Thailand, is a basic ingredient of many Thai curries, is available in cans, cartons and as a powder.

With a delicate lemon flavour, LEMONGRASS looks like a giant scallion. When finely chopped, the lower stalk is eaten, but bigger pieces are only for flavouring.

GALANGAL, called *kah* in Thailand, is pounded into a paste and used in creating virtually all curry pastes. Sliced, it is also used to flavour a variety of other dishes.

The fresh leaves and dried seeds of the CORIANDER plant are popular everywhere. The Thais, however, stand alone in also using the roots in their cooking.

Three types of fresh BASIL are used in Thai cooking. *Bai grapaow* – sometimes called holy basil – has an intense flavour and appears only to be eaten in Thailand. *Bai horapa* has a strong anise flavor and *bai mangluk* has a mild lemony taste.

The leaves of the KAFFIR LIME tree and zest of its fruit are used extensively.

KAPI, a paste made from fermented shrimp, is an essential ingredient in Thai cooking. Everyone agrees it smells horrible, but tastes good when cooked.

The liquid obtained by soaking the pulp of the TAMARIND pod is used to give a tart flavour to many Thai dishes.

A
B
C
D
E
F
H
I
J
K
L
M
N
N
N
O

UTENSILS

USED IN THAI COOKING

Thai kitchens are simple and sparsely furnished. Very few utensils are used to prepare a Thai meal, and most have been around for a long time. The most notable exception is the electric rice cooker, a bit of modern technology that can be found in virtually every Thai home possessing electricity.

A mortar and pestle hewn from granite is used to make the curry pastes needed in most Thai dishes. A round chopping block fashioned from the trunk or branch of a tamarind tree is another basic necessity. The cutting and chopping done on this block is usually performed with a durable Chinese-style cleaver. A small cheap knife with a stainless steel blade is used for most peeling and trimming.

A wok, called a *katha* in Thailand, is the one cooking vessel that is universal. Although spun steel models like those found in China are common, woks fashioned from aluminum are equally popular. Many cooks use cheap aluminum pots for making curries, but many still use unglazed clay pots like those used in Thailand for centuries. The more affluent are likely to use thin stainless steel pots that are easier to clean. Many cooks have a large stainless steel spatula that they use with their wok, but this is by no means universal. All seem to have a collection of spoons and other implements made from wood that they use for stirring, ladling and dipping.

These are the most common basic utensils found in a Thai kitchen. Other items are often used, depending upon the affluence and idiosyncrasies of the chef.

- **A** Ladle for skimming soups & curries
- **B** Ladle used with a wok
- **C** Chinese style cleaver
- **D** Tamarind wood chopping block
- **E** Pan for cooking certain desserts, such as *khanom krok*
- **F** Brass Wok (*katha thong*) – for making special desserts
- **G** Typical strainer used for removing items from boiling water or hot oil
- **H** Clay pot (*maw din*) for cooking over charcoal
- **I** Wok, called a *katha* in Thai
- **J** Bamboo brush for cleaning a wok
- **K** **L** Varieties of strainer & ladle
- **M** Traditional stainless steel spatula used in cooking with a wok
- **N** Varieties of wooden spatulas & ladles
- **O** Mortar and pestle hewn from granite

Chef Theerati's Recommended Menus

Thai food is meant to be shared. The best way to enjoy your Thai meal is to place a number of dishes on the table for all to try.

One of the features of Thai food is that certain dishes are complementary, giving a superb balance between sweet and sour, rich and light, salt and sour.

To help you plan your Thai meals while you gain experience at putting together your own menus, we present four suggested menus, one or the other suitable for practically every occasion.

Traditionally in Thailand, soup would be served as part of the main course and eaten at the same time. However, we have shown soup as a separate course in our menus. Additionally, while most meals would be served with steamed rice, we have added fried rice to three of the menus for a more varied choice.

The Andaman Catch

A wonderful selection of seafood using ingredients that would normally be caught in the waters around the island of Phuket.

A great wintertime lunch or summertime dinner menu, these dishes would be eaten by Thais from Phuket going out as a family or a group of friends.

The Family Feast

An ideal informal lunch or dinner menu for family or friends. Throughout Thailand, this is the type of menu that might be cooked at home, probably over the weekend, or to celebrate a really special family occasion.

Poo Cha — PAGE 36
Deep fried crab in a golden nest

Tom Yam Goong — PAGE 56
Spicy shrimp and lemongrass soup

Moo Tod Gratiem Prik Thai — PAGE 70
Fried pork with garlic and black pepper

Hoi Ma Laeng Poo — PAGE 84
Fresh mussels with chili sauce

Gaeng Khiaow Waan Goong — PAGE 98
Green curry with shrimps

Khao Phad Goong — PAGE 112
Fried rice with shrimps

Phad Pak Ruam Naam Man Hoi — PAGE 116
Stir-fried mixed vegetables in oyster sauce

Tub Tim Grob — PAGE 126
Jellied water chestnuts in syrup with crushed ice

The Four Corners of Thailand

This celebration menu pulls together dishes from the fourcorners of Thailand, and is the sort of meal that would be eaten as a celebration dinner in a wealthy Thai household. It is the perfect sumptuous menu to introduce friends to the varied tastes of Thailand – and to your expertise in reproducing them.

The Sukhothai

Although this book is about Thai Country Cooking, it would be remiss to ignore the delights of Royal Thai Cuisine (once served only in the Royal Thai Household). Dishes featured here are reminiscent of the days of Old Siam; this sort of menu graces tables throughout Thailand, for such occasions as a very special Sunday lunch or an important dinner party.

Appetizers

Dishes featured in this section may properly be called appetizers, although in Thailand there is often no clear distinction in the order various dishes are served. You might want to serve them as appetizers in the western sense, as cocktail snacks or simply as another dish on the table.

Thai country food lacks formality, leaving the style of service up to you.

Gai Hor Bai Toey

Chicken Cooked in Pandanus Leaves

Ingredients

300 gm chicken breast
1 tbsp white soya sauce
1/2 tsp sesame oil
1 pch sugar
1 tbsp Thai rice wine
30 gm wheat flour
1 clove garlic (finely chopped)
1 tsp fresh coriander (finely chopped)
Ground black pepper to taste
7 pandanus leaves

For the sesame sauce

60 gm sugar
10 gm tomato ketchup
2 tbsp chili sauce
2 tbsp white vinegar
2 tsp grated ginger
2 tsp toasted sesame seeds
4 tbsp soya sauce
100 ml water

- Mix ingredients together by hand; place in suitable dish.

Preparation

- Cut the chicken breast into 2cm cubes & marinade with all the ingredients for at least one hour.
- Fold each chicken piece into a pandanus leaf to form a parcel (see photo opposite & diagram on p134).
- Steam the chicken parcel for about 7 minutes.
- Remove, drain & deep fry in hot oil.
- Remove & place on a piece of kitchen paper (strong tissue) to allow oil to drain off.
- Serve hot with sesame sauce separately.

Options

You may substitute leek for pandanus leaf, though this will weaken the flavours.

MOO SARONG

Wrapped Minced Pork with Egg Noodles

Ingredients

200 gm pork loin (minced)
150 gm yellow noodles
3 eggs
1 tbsp coriander (finely chopped)
3-4 cloves garlic (chopped)
1 tbsp soya sauce
Ground black pepper to taste
Fresh coriander leaves to garnish
Sweet plum sauce

Preparation

- Season minced pork with garlic, coriander, soya sauce & pepper. Mix with eggs.
- Roll mixture into 2cm balls.
- Wrap the pork balls in the yellow noodles.
- Steam for 3 minutes, then deep fry in vegetable oil.
- Garnish with coriander leaf.
- Serve hot with sweet plum sauce separately.

Options

For this dish, you may substitute minced chicken or shrimp for pork.

TOD MAN GOONG

Deep Fried Shrimp Patties with Sweet Plum Sauce

Ingredients

150 gm white shrimps
1 egg
1 clove garlic (chopped)
5 gm coriander (finely chopped)
1 tbsp oyster sauce
1 tsp sugar
1 tsp white soy sauce
1/3 tsp seasoning soy sauce (Maggi)
1/3 tsp sesame oil
20 gm breadcrumbs
40 gm minced pork fat or lard
Ground black pepper to taste
Sweet plum sauce

Preparation

- Peel, de-vein & mince the shrimps. Mix minced shrimp meat well with all ingredients.
- Form into small patties (see photograph opposite).
- Coat in breadcrumbs & deep fry in hot oil until golden brown.
- Serve hot with sweet plum sauce separately.

Options

You may substitute minced white fishmeat for shrimp. The dish is then called *Tod Man Pla*.

POO CHA

Deep Fried Crab in a Golden Nest

Ingredients

200 gm crabmeat
120 gm minced pork
2 eggs
2 cloves garlic (chopped)
1 tsp ground coriander root
10 gm onion (chopped)
2 crab shells
1 red chili (seeded & sliced) to garnish
Ground black pepper to taste
Sweet plum sauce

Preparation

- Mix the minced pork, crabmeat & one egg until well blended.
- Add garlic, onion, coriander root & seasoning; mix well.
- Place mixture into the crab shells.
- Steam for 3-5 minutes.
- Dip in beaten egg & deep fry for 2-3 minutes.
- Garnish with red chili.
- Serve hot with plum sauce separately.

Options

If you prefer, replace the pork with an additional 150 gm of crabmeat.

KHAO TANG SAVOEY

Rice Crackers with a Curry-Shrimp Sauce

Ingredients

5 dried rice crackers
4 large white shrimps
30 ml coconut milk (fresh or canned)
5 gm coriander roots (finely chopped)
3-4 cloves garlic (chopped)
1 tsp red curry paste
1 tsp sugar
1 tbsp fish sauce
Fresh coriander leaves to garnish

Preparation

- Deep fry the rice crackers until light golden brown. Take care not to overcook.
- Peel, de-vein & chop the white shrimps.
- Prepare the sauce by sautéeing the shrimps, together with the garlic, coriander & curry paste.
- Add coconut milk; simmer sauce until slightly thickened.
- Add sugar & fish sauce to taste.
- Garnish with fresh coriander leaves.
- Serve the sauce hot, separately from the rice crackers.

Helpful Tip

Test cook a few rice crackers in advance of your dinner party. Have some spare in stock in case of overcooking.

GOONG KRABOK

Deep Fried Shrimps in Spring Roll Skins

Ingredients

80 gm large shrimps
3 spring roll skins
50 gm yambeans
30 gm celery
Salt & ground black pepper to taste
Sweet plum sauce

Preparation

- Peel the shrimps (keep the tails on) & de-vein.
- Season & wrap in the spring roll skin.
- Deep fry in hot oil until golden-brown, crisp & well cooked.
- Arrange on suitable platter with garnish.
- Serve hot with sweet plum sauce separately.

Comments

Simple to prepare, this dish is a favourite snack for before the main meal. Preparing a garnish of your choice offers a good opportunity to practice your vegetable carving skills.

SALADS

Thai salads are often a surprise to Western palates. Unlike in the West, raw vegetables do not feature as a significant component. The common traits in Thai salads are chili and lime juice, the resulting dish being spicy and tart. Sometimes warm, sometimes cold, Thai salads are always a refreshing part of the meal, providing a superb contrast with rich dishes that incorporate coconut milk.

LARB GAI

Spicy Minced Chicken Salad with Fresh Mint

Ingredients

200 gm chicken breast (minced)
40 gm shallots (peeled & thinly sliced)
20 gm parsley (chopped)
20 gm spring onion (thinly sliced)
2 tbsp rice (toasted & ground)
1 tbsp dried chili
2 tbsp fresh lime juice
2 tbsp fish sauce
1/2 cup of water
Fresh mint leaves to garnish

Preparation

- Sautée the minced chicken in a wok.
- Add 1/2 a cup of water to complete the cooking. Remove from the heat.
- Mix all the vegetables and season with the dried chili powder, fish sauce & lime juice.
- Toast the rice in a heavy pan, then grind until it has a coarsely chopped appearance.
- Add the rice & chicken to the salad, mix & garnish with the mint leaves.

Options

To vary this recipe, you may substitute ground pork for the chicken. The dish is then called *Larb Moo.*

PLA GOONG NANG

Spicy Shrimp Salad with Lemongrass & Chili

Ingredients

12 large, fresh white shrimps
50 gm shallots (peeled & sliced)
2 small hot chilies
2 whole lemongrass (very thinly sliced)
2 kaffir lime leaves (very thinly sliced)
Fresh mint leaves to garnish

For the dressing

2 tbsp fish sauce
2 tbsp fresh lime juice
1 tbsp roasted chili paste (*nam prik pao*)

- Combine lime juice, fish sauce & chili paste.

Preparation

- Peel & de-vein the shrimps.
- Poach the shrimps in water & marinade in the dressing.
- Combine all the remaining ingredients, add the shrimps & toss in the dressing.
- Serve garnished with mint leaves.

Options

You may replace the kaffir lime leaves with fresh lime zest, but you will lose some of the intensity. This dish, when cooked by Thais, is especially spicy. Vary the amount of chili if you prefer your Thai salad a little milder.

YAM WOON SEN

Glass Noodle Salad with Pork & Shrimps

Ingredients

100 gm jelly vermicelli
100 gm shrimps
70 gm minced pork
4 cloves pickled garlic (sliced)
40 gm shallots (peeled & sliced)
20 gm fungus mushrooms (sliced)
10 gm dried shrimps
2 tbsp fish sauce
2 tbsp fresh lime juice
1 large red chili to garnish
Fresh coriander leaves to garnish
40 gm spring onions to garnish

Preparation

- Boil the vermicelli briefly, remove from heat & refresh in cold water. Set aside.
- Peel & de-vein shrimps. Poach in water & set aside.
- Steam the minced pork & set aside.
- Mix the garlic, shallots, dried shrimps & mushrooms together with the lime juice & fish sauce.
- Add the cooked shrimps & pork; mix well.
- Add to the vermicelli; toss well but briefly.
- Serve garnished with the spring onion, coriander leaves & chili.

Helpful tip

Be very careful not to overcook the vermicelli. It should be tender but not 'soggy'. A minute is usually enough.

YAM TALAY

Spicy Seafood Salad

Ingredients

100 gm squid
5 medium shrimps
80 gm snapper (filleted)
70 gm mussels (shelled)
70 gm onion (thinly sliced)
40 gm celery (thinly sliced)
50 gm tomato (seeded & sliced)
Fresh coriander & salad leaves to garnish

For the dressing

10 gm small hot chili (chopped)
2 tbsp fish sauce
2 tbsp fresh lime juice
2 tbsp chili sauce

- Combine lime juice, fish sauce & chili sauce with the chopped hot chili.

Preparation

- Peel & de-vein shrimps. Clean & slice squid. Cut the snapper into finger-sized slices.
- Poach the seafood items separately. Set aside.
- Toss the vegetables in the dressing, then add the cooked seafood & mix.
- Serve on the salad leaves & garnish with fresh coriander leaves.

Helpful tip

This dish can be served while the seafood is still warm, or after cooling. If you want to serve it warm, make sure all preparation is completed before poaching the seafood.

YAM NEUA YANG

GRILLED BEEF SALAD WITH LIME DRESSING

INGREDIENTS

180 gm sirloin steak
70 gm onion (thinly sliced)
40 gm celery (thinly sliced)
50 gm tomato (seeded & sliced)
30 gm spring onion (sliced)
20 gm cucumber (peeled & sliced)
Fresh coriander & salad leaves to garnish

FOR THE DRESSING

10 gm small hot chili (chopped)
2 tbsp fish sauce
2 tbsp fresh lime juice
2 tbsp chili sauce
1/2 tsp sugar

➤ Combine lime juice, fish sauce & chili sauce with the chopped hot chili.

PREPARATION

➤ Grill the sirloin until medium rare. Slice & set aside.

➤ Toss the vegetables in the dressing, then add the sirloin & mix.

➤ Serve on the salad leaves; garnish with fresh coriander leaves & decorate with sliced cucumber.

HELPFUL TIP

This dish can be served while the beef is still warm, or after cooling. If you want to serve it warm, leave grilling the steak until all other preparation is complete.

SOUPS

Unlike in the West, soups in Thailand are not considered as a starter. They are a significant part of the meal, providing an important balance between fried or grilled food (dry), curries (thick and often sweet) and delicate (steamed) dishes. The choice of soup depends on other dishes selected.

Thai soups may be sharp and sour (*Tom Yam*), rich and fragrant (*Tom Kha*), or 'clean' and simple (*Gaeng Jurd*). Whatever the soup, you will find that the herbs and spices used to provide the unique flavours are all left in the pot when the soup is served.

Tom Yam Goong

Spicy Shrimp & Lemongrass Soup

Ingredients

6 medium white shrimps
350 ml chicken stock
15 gm shallots (peeled & sliced)
15 gm galangal (chopped)
20 gm lemongrass (sliced)
15 gm small hot chilies (whole)
20 gm straw mushrooms (cut in halves)
10 kaffir lime leaves
1 tbsp roasted chili paste
Fresh lemon juice
1 tsp fish sauce
Fresh coriander leaves to garnish

Preparation

- Peel & de-vein the shrimps. Set aside.
- Gently sautée the galangal, roasted chili paste, shallots, lemongrass & chilies to release their flavours.
- Cover with chicken stock & add the shrimps, mushrooms & fish sauce to taste. Simmer gently for 2 minutes.
- Add the kaffir lime leaves & adjust the flavour with the lemon juice. (*Tom Yam* should be spicy, fresh & tangy – how tangy depends on how you like it & on how much lemon juice you use. Experiment!)
- Sprinkle the coriander leaves on top to garnish.

Options

You may substitute diced chicken for the shrimps. The dish is then called *Tom Yam Gai*.

TOM KHA GAI

Chicken & Coconut Milk Soup with Thai Herbs

Ingredients

80 gm chicken breast
200 ml chicken stock
20 gm straw mushrooms
200 ml coconut milk
20 gm lemongrass (sliced)
20 gm shallots (peeled & sliced)
20 gm galangal root (sliced into 'coins')
20 gm coriander roots (sliced)
10 gm dried chilies
Juice of 1 lime
1 tbsp fish sauce
10 kaffir lime leaves (shredded)
Fresh coriander leaves to garnish

Preparation

- Cut the chicken breast into 1-2cm cubes. Set aside.
- Lightly sautée the galangal, coriander roots, shallots, chili & lemongrass to release their aromas.
- Add the mushrooms & cook for a further 1 minute, stirring occasionally.
- Pour in the chicken stock & coconut milk. Bring to a gentle simmer for 2 minutes.
- Season the broth with the lime juice, half the shredded lime leaves & fish sauce to taste.
- Add the diced chicken & cook in the liquid gently for 2 minutes (the chicken will become tough if overcooked).
- Serve with the remaining shredded kaffir lime leaves on top, together with coriander leaves, as garnish.

Gaeng Liang Noppakoaw

Thai Gourd & Shrimp Soup

Ingredients

4 medium white shrimps
70 gm pumpkin (peeled & diced)
30 gm gourd (peeled & diced)
20 gm carrots (peeled & sliced)
500 ml chicken stock
40 gm shallots (peeled & sliced)
1/8 bunch morning gourd leaves (*tumlurng*)
10 white basil leaves (*bai mang luk*)
30 gm *nung fa* mushrooms (steamed)
Salt & sugar to taste

For the shrimp paste

20 gm dried shrimps
1 tsp shrimp paste
5 gm black peppercorns
20 gm coriander root

- Grind or pound the coriander root, dried shrimp, shrimp paste & black peppercorns, until smooth.

Preparation

- Peel & de-vein the shrimps. Set aside.
- Heat the chicken stock & flavour with the shrimp paste mixture.
- Add the pumpkin, carrot & gourd to the stock; simmer slowly for 5 minutes. Add the white shrimps & simmer for another 2 minutes.
- Finish with the morning gourd leaves, white basil, mushrooms & shallots & serve immediately.

Options

You may use English spinach instead of gourd leaves, & cucumber instead of gourd.

GAENG JURD SEAFOOD SARAI TALAY

CLEAR SEAFOOD SOUP WITH SEAWEED

INGREDIENTS

3 medium white shrimps (peeled & de-veined)
50 gm barracuda fillet (diced)
70 gm squid (diced)
500 ml chicken stock
10 gm seaweed (washed)
30 gm spring onion (finely sliced)
30 gm celery (chopped)
1-2 cloves garlic (finely chopped)
1 tbsp white soy sauce
Ground black pepper to taste

PREPARATION

- Peel & de-vein the shrimps. Set aside.
- Fry the chopped garlic in oil until golden brown & crispy. Set aside.
- Lightly steam the barracuda, squid & shrimps. Place in soup bowls or a serving dish & add the prepared celery, spring onion & seaweed.
- Bring the chicken stock to the boil. Season with the pepper & soy sauce.
- Pour the hot liquid over the seafood.
- Sprinkle the fried garlic on top & serve.

OPTIONS

If barracuda is not available, substitute a locally available, firm-fleshed fish such as snapper or sea bass.

MEAT DISHES

In the West meat – often big slabs of it – forms the major part of a meal. Roast lamb, T-bone steaks, pork chops, mixed grills... these dishes represent the norm in western food. Even in the more esoteric French and Italian cuisines, main dishes are usually based on one large piece of meat.

Not so in Thailand. While few dishes are without some form of meat or seafood – indeed vegetarians may have a hard time in Thailand – even the specifically 'meat' dishes are based only on quite small amounts of minced, diced or sliced meats.

Thais will usually eat small amounts of several meat dishes during a meal.

PHAD GRAPAOW MOO

STIR FRIED PORK WITH GARLIC & HOT BASIL

INGREDIENTS

200 gm porkloin (minced)
6-7 cloves fresh garlic (finely chopped)
10 gm small hot chilies (whole)
20 gm medium chili (sliced)
1 tbsp oyster sauce
1 tbsp fish sauce
Ground black pepper & sugar to taste
Small bunch hot basil leaves

PREPARATION

- Fry the chopped garlic in oil until golden brown & crispy, but not burnt. Set aside.
- Sautée the pork using the oil from frying the garlic.
- Add the chilies & season with the oyster sauce, black pepper, fried garlic & sugar.
- Add the hot basil leaves before serving.

OPTIONS

This dish can be served with 10 medium prawns (peeled, de-veined & chopped) or 200 gm minced chicken instead of the pork. The dishes are then called *Phad Grapaow Goong* and *Phad Grapaow Gai* respectively.

NEUA PHAD NAAM MAN HOI

STIR FRIED BEEF WITH OYSTER SAUCE

INGREDIENTS

200 gm topside of beef
70 gm straw mushrooms
30 gm onion (peeled & sliced)
20 gm spring onions (sliced)
15 gm medium chilies (split & sliced)
3-4 cloves garlic (chopped)
2 tbsp oyster sauce
1 tbsp white soya sauce
1 gm fresh ginger (peeled and thinly sliced)
Ground black pepper to taste
White flour for 'dusting'

PREPARATION

- Cut the beef into small 'finger-sized' pieces & marinade in half the black pepper & white soya sauce for 10 minutes.
- Remove from marinade, lightly dust with flour & deep fry quickly until the outside is crispy (make sure the oil is hot before you start).
- Pre-heat a wok until medium hot. Add a small quantity of oil & stir fry the onions, garlic, chili & ginger, adding the beef in the final stages.
- Season with the oyster sauce, white soya sauce & remaining black pepper. Add the spring onions & serve.

OPTIONS

Omit the chili if you prefer, especially if other dishes in your menu are very spicy.

MOO TOD GRATIEM PRIK THAI

FRIED PORK WITH GARLIC & BLACK PEPPER

INGREDIENTS

200 gm porkloin
8-10 cloves garlic (chopped)
1 tbsp oyster sauce
1 tbsp white soya sauce
1 tsp ground black pepper
White flour for 'dusting'
Fresh coriander leaves to garnish

PREPARATION

- Fry the garlic in hot oil until golden brown & crispy, but not burnt. Set aside.
- Cut the meat into small 'finger-sized' pieces & marinate in the white soya sauce & half the black pepper.
- Dust in flour & fry in hot oil until crispy.
- Combine the meat in a pre-heated wok with the oyster sauce, crispy garlic & remaining black pepper.
- Remove from heat as soon as thoroughly mixed.
- Serve garnished with the fresh coriander leaves.

OPTIONS

This dish can be made with prawns (10 medium prawns), chicken breast (200 gm) or squid (200 gm) instead of pork. The dish is called *Goong, Gai* and *Pla Meuk Tod Gratiem Prik Thai* respectively.

GAI PHAD MED MAMUANG HIMAPAAN

FRIED CHICKEN WITH CASHEW NUTS

INGREDIENTS

180 gm chicken breast
40 gm onion (diced)
70 gm cashew nuts
60 gm (1/4 can) straw mushrooms
10 gm dried red chilies (sliced)
20 gm spring onions (sliced)
20 gm water chestnuts (whole)
1 tbsp oyster sauce
1 tbsp white soya sauce
1 tbsp roasted chili paste in oil
Ground black pepper to taste
White flour for 'dusting'

PREPARATION

- Toast the cashew nuts until light golden brown. Set aside.
- Slice the straw mushrooms. Set aside.
- Cut the chicken into small 'finger-sized' pieces, dust in flour & deep fry in hot oil until crispy.
- Pre-heat a wok, adding a little oil; fry the dried chili, then add the onions, mushrooms & water chestnuts.
- Stir fry & season with the chili paste, soya sauce, oyster sauce & black pepper.
- Add the cashew nuts & spring onions, mix with the chicken & serve.

GAI OB MANAO

LIME MARINATED ROAST CHICKEN

INGREDIENTS

400 gm chicken breast
2 tbsp freshly squeezed lime juice
10 gm butter
50 gm kale
3-4 cloves garlic (chopped)
2 tbsp sugar
Salt & ground black pepper to taste
White flour for 'dusting'

PREPARATION

- Marinade the chicken breast in the salt, black pepper, sugar & lime juice for 20 minutes.
- Lightly dust the marinated chicken in flour & brown in a heavy skillet with the butter.
- Place in an oven set at 150°C & cook for about 8-10 minutes, until the chicken is cooked through, but still tender.
- Slice and deep-fry the kale leaves.
- To serve, slice the chicken breast & place on the fried kale leaves.

OPTIONS

You may use a whole chicken instead of chicken breast. In this case, allow more time for marinating, ensuring that the chicken flesh is in contact with the marinade at all times.

SEAFOOD DISHES

Thailand is blessed with a fantastically long coastline for the size of the country, a blessing that has had a huge influence on the country's cuisine.

Seafood is abundant in all shapes and sizes, from mouth-watering jumbo prawns, to aphrodisiacal fresh oysters, from tender fleshed snapper to blue crab – and many more. Coupled with the profusion of cooking methods, herbs, spices and sauces available to Thai chefs, seafood is the jewel in the crown of Thai cuisine.

TALAY PHAD KREUNG TESS

STIR FRIED SEAFOOD WITH THAI HERBS

INGREDIENTS

70 gm white shrimps
70 gm squid
120 gm snapper fillet – or other similar fish
100 gm mussels in 1/2-shell
50 gm cockles in 1/2-shell
8 cloves garlic (chopped)
20 gm galangal (peeled & sliced)
2 small hot chilies (chopped)
10 hot basil leaves
1 tbsp black soya sauce
2 tbsp white soya sauce
2 tbsp oyster sauce
Ground black pepper to taste
White flour for 'dusting'

PREPARATION

Prepare seafood as described below & set aside:

- Peel & de-vein the shrimps. Clean & slice the squid.
- Steam the mussels & cockles for 2-3 minutes.
- Cut snapper fillet into finger-sized pieces &lightly dust with flour. Deep fry until golden brown.

- Heat a wok until medium hot; fry the garlic & galangal; add the seafood & chili, seasoning with oyster sauce, soya sauce & black pepper.
- Stir fry for 2-3 minutes until the seafood is cooked, adding black soya sauce for colour.
- Add the hot basil leaves & fried snapper, toss & serve.

OPTIONS

You may replace any of the seafood above with your personal favourites.

POO MA PHAD PONG GAREE

STIR-FRIED BLUE CRAB WITH YELLOW CURRY

INGREDIENTS

400 gm blue crab
3-4 cloves garlic (chopped)
1 egg (beaten)
2 tsp curry powder
1 tbsp chili paste in oil
1/2 cup milk
30 gm onions (sliced)
2 tbsp white soya sauce
1 tbsp oyster sauce
Salt & ground black pepper to taste
White flour for 'dusting'

SLICED, FOR GARNISH

- 20 gm red chilies
- 30 gm celery
- 30 gm spring onions

PREPARATION

- Prepare the blue crabs by removing the shells, cleaning & cutting into 4 pieces.
- Season with the salt & half the pepper, then lightly dust in flour.
- Deep fry in hot oil until golden & crispy. Set aside.
- Combine the milk, eggs & chili paste in oil with the curry powder. Set aside.
- In a wok, sautée the onions & garlic with the cooked crab; add the egg mixture, stirring constantly.
- Remove from the heat & set aside to allow the eggs to complete cooking.
- Season with the oyster sauce, soya sauce & remaining pepper.
- Serve, garnished with the chili, celery & spring onions.

OPTIONS

You may replace blue crabs with your favourite shellfish.

PLA PRIAOW WAAN

Fried Fish in Sweet & Sour Sauce

Ingredients

200 gm fish fillet (snapper or similar)
10 gm wheat flour
10 ml white soya sauce
White pepper to taste
10 gm spring onions to garnish
White flour for 'dusting'

For the sweet & sour sauce

50 gm onions (diced)
50 gm tomatoes (diced)
30 gm salad cucumber (diced)
50 gm pineapple (diced)
20 gm tomato ketchup
1 tbsp white vinegar
1 tsp white sugar
Salt & ground black pepper to taste

- Sautée the onion first, then add the remaining vegetables, ketchup & vinegar. Simmer for about 4 minutes.

Preparation

- Cut fish fillet into finger-sized pieces. Season, lightly dust with flour & fry in oil until crispy.
- Arrange the fried fish on a plate & pour the sauce over. Garnish with spring onion & serve.

Options

You may replace the fish fillet with prawns or any meat of your choice.

HOI MA LAENG POO

Fresh Mussels with Chili Sauce

Ingredients

1 kg fresh mussels
10 ml chicken stock
10 gm spring onions (finely chopped)
10 gm celery (diced)
1 clove garlic (finely chopped)
1 whole red chili (sliced)
1 tbsp oyster sauce
1 tbsp red curry paste
1 tbsp fish sauce
1 tsp sugar
5 gm cornflour
Fresh sweet basil leaves to garnish

Preparation

- Heat a large pot, add a little oil & quickly fry the garlic, celery & chili paste.
- Add the mussels & sautée for 1 minute.
- Pour on the chicken stock & add the rest of the ingredients (excluding the basil leaves).
- Cover the pot & simmer for a good 6 minutes, until all mussels are open.
- Mix the cornflour with a little water & add slowly to the sauce, stirring continuously until the sauce thickens.
- Decorate with the fresh basil leaves and serve.

GOONG OB GLUEA

Baked Casserole of Prawns

Ingredients

8 medium white prawns
3-4 cloves garlic (roughly chopped)
10 gm ginger (peeled & sliced)
20 gm pork fat (cut in strips)
20 gm coriander roots (chopped)
2 tsp white soya sauce
1 tsp oyster sauce
Salt & ground black pepper to taste
Fresh coriander & lettuce leaves to garnish

Preparation

- Peel & de-vein, then 'butterfly cut' the prawns. Season with half the soya sauce & lightly dust in flour. (See page 134 for tips on 'butterfly cutting')
- Quickly deep fry the prawns until crispy.
- Heat a wok to medium heat; sautée the pork fat, garlic, ginger & coriander roots.
- Add the cooked prawns & flavour with oyster sauce, white soya sauce & crushed black pepper.
- Cover the wok & simmer until the shrimps are completely cooked.
- Lay the lettuce leaves in a casserole dish, fill with the shrimps & garnish with coriander leaves.

GANG MUNGKORN PHAD NAAM MAKARM

LOBSTER IN TAMARIND SAUCE

INGREDIENTS

500 gm lobster (split & cleaned)
20 gm shallots (peeled & chopped)
2-3 cloves garlic (chopped)
5 gm red chilies (split & seeded)
1 tbsp white soya sauce
1 tbsp seasoning soya sauce (Maggi)
5 gm cornflour
Ground black pepper to taste
White flour for 'dusting'
Fresh coriander leaves to garnish

FOR THE TAMARIND SAUCE

1 tbsp palm sugar (or soft brown sugar)
30 gm tamarind (pulp)
Salt to taste

- Soak the tamarind in lukewarm water, squeezing the fruit to extract the pulp. Discard the shell. Boil pulp for 3 minutes, then add palm sugar & salt.

PREPARATION

- Remove lobster meat from the shell; set shell aside.
- Cut lobster meat into cubes, dust in flour & deep fry until crispy.
- Heat a wok; add the oil, shallots, red chili, lobster & tamarind sauce.
- Mix the cornflour with a little water & add slowly to the sauce, stirring continuously until it thickens.
- To serve, place the cooked lobster & sauce into the hollowed-out shell; garnish with coriander leaves.

PLA NEUNG MANAO

Steamed Whole Fish in Lime Dressing

Ingredients

1 whole snapper
1 tbsp vegetable oil
3 shallots (sliced)
2 cloves garlic (chopped)
1 piece of ginger (sliced)
2 whole red chilies (sliced)
20 ml lime juice
2 tbsp fish sauce
2 lemon leaves
1 whole lime (sliced)
Salt & ground black pepper to taste
Fresh coriander leaves to garnish

Preparation

- Clean the fish, wash thoroughly with plain water. Dry with a kitchen towel (strong tissue).
- Make a marinade with all the remaining ingredients.
- Place the fish on a large platter & marinade for 30 minutes.
- Leaving the marinade in place, cover & steam over boiling water for approximately 25 minutes.
- Serve directly, garnished with coriander leaves & the sliced lime.

Options

If snapper is not available, you can use any other whole, white-fleshed fish.

Curries

'Curry' is something of a misnomer for a range of dishes that includes the thick, hot, dry *Panang*, the creamy, sweet *Gaeng Khiaow Waan*, and the blisteringly hot, soup-like *Gaeng Som*.

Going even further, some Thai curries are hot and sweet, others hot and sour, others still surprisingly mild. Thai curries share no common ingredients, other than some form of curry paste mixed with herbs and chili in varying quantities.

Probably the most widely recognised form of Thai curry is generic *gaeng gratik*, where coconut milk is the unifying ingredient. Yet, as you will find when you try the Thai curries in this section, that is just the starting point.

GAENG GAREE GAI

YELLOW CHICKEN CURRY

INGREDIENTS

200 gm chicken breast
50 ml chicken stock
60 gm potatoes (roughly chopped)
40 gm onion (chopped)
1/3 large can coconut milk
1 tbsp yellow curry paste
1 tsp sugar
1 pch red chili slivers
Salt to taste

PREPARATION

- Cut the chicken into thick slices. Set aside.
- Blanche the potatoes in boiling water. Set aside.
- Heat a little oil in a wok. Stir fry the onion until golden brown, then add the curry paste & continue frying for 1 minute.
- Pour in the chicken stock & the coconut milk.
- Add the chicken breast & simmer for a good 3 minutes.
- Add the blanched potatoes & continue to simmer for a further 5 minutes.
- Decorate with sliced red chili slivers & serve.

GAENG MUSSAMAN NEUA
MUSLIM-STYLE BEEF CURRY

INGREDIENTS

180 gm top side of beef (cubed)
50 ml chicken stock
1/2 large can coconut milk
50 gm onion (chopped)
3-4 cloves garlic (chopped)
100 gm potatoes (roughly chopped)
1 tbsp mussaman curry paste
1 cinnamon stick
5 gm star anise
5 gm cardamom
1 tsp palm sugar
1 tbsp fish sauce
20 gm roasted peanuts

PREPARATION

- Heat a little oil in a wok. Stir fry the onion & garlic until golden brown, then add the curry paste & continue frying for 1 minute.
- Pour in the chicken stock & the coconut milk, adding the cubed beef, cinnamon stick, cardamom, star anise & fish sauce.
- Simmer for about 1 hour.
- Add the potatoes & simmer for a further 20 minutes.
- Add the roasted peanuts & serve.

OPTIONS

Mussaman-style curry is as often made with chicken as with beef. Cut chicken breast into thick slices. Blanche the potatoes in advance & reduce the cooking times to those for *Gaeng Garee Gai* (p95).

GAENG KHIAOW WAAN GOONG

GREEN CURRY WITH SHRIMPS

INGREDIENTS

100 gm white shrimps
1 cup chicken stock
1/3 large can coconut milk
1 tbsp green curry paste
30 gm small green eggplant (quartered)
2 kaffir lime leaves (shredded)
20 gm red chilies (sliced)
1 tsp sugar
Fresh sweet basil leaves to garnish

PREPARATION

- Heat a little oil in a wok. Fry the green curry paste, adding the sugar, coconut milk & chicken stock. Bring to the boil.
- Add the shrimps to the sauce & simmer for a good 3 minutes on medium heat.
- Add the chili, eggplant & kaffir lime leaves. Cook for another 2-3 minutes.
- Garnish with the sweet basil leaves & serve.

OPTIONS

If you are unable to find small green eggplant, you can replace with regular purple eggplant.

Gaeng Khiaow Waan is very popular made with chicken instead of shrimps. Cut chicken breast into thick slices. Increase the cooking time to ensure the chicken is well cooked.

PANANG MOO

Panang-Style Pork Curry

Ingredients

200 gm pork loin
1 tbsp panang curry paste
1/3 large can coconut milk
40 gm roasted peanuts (ground)
1 tsp sugar
Salt to taste

For garnish

2 kaffir lime leaves (shredded)
1 red chili (sliced)

Preparation

- Cut pork into finger-sized strips. Fry briefly until sealed on the outside. Set aside.
- Heat a little oil in a wok. Fry the curry paste, then add about 2/3 of the coconut milk, sugar & salt.
- Add the pork & simmer for a good 20 minutes, adding a little water as necessary to keep the sauce from drying out completely. (Panang-style curry should be thick & creamy, but not 'liquid'.)
- Add the ground peanuts & stir thoroughly.
- Simmer the remaining coconut milk until it reduces to about half the volume & pour on top.
- Garnish with red chili & kaffir lime leaves & serve.

Options

Panang curry is equally popular made with chicken instead of pork. Cut chicken breast into thick slices, & follow the instructions above.

GAENG PHET PED YANG

RED CURRY WITH ROAST DUCK & GRAPES

INGREDIENTS

1 whole duck
1/4 large can coconut milk
40 gm grapes
30 gm cherry tomato (whole)
30 gm pineapple (cubed)
1 tbsp red chili paste
2 kaffir lime leaves (shredded)
20 gm red chilies (sliced)
40 gm sugar
2 tbsp fish sauce

FOR GARNISH

1 whole red chili
Fresh sweet basil leaves

PREPARATION

- Roast the duck in the oven, de-bone & slice into finger-sized pieces. Set aside.
- Heat a little oil in a wok. Briefly fry the red chili paste, adding the sliced chilies, coconut milk, sugar, fish sauce & kaffir lime leaves. Simmer for about 2 minutes.
- Add the duck meat & simmer until the meat is hot.
- Add the pineapple, cherry tomatoes & grapes just before serving.
- Serve, garnished with the sweet basil leaves & whole red chili.

OPTIONS

You may substitute any poultry for the roast duck.

Perrier
Nasta

Rice & Noodle Dishes

Rice and noodles are the two 'staples' in the Thai diet. But this does not necessarily mean that they are interchangeable, or that they represent the same to Thais as, for example, potatoes do to westerners.

Plain rice – *Khao Suay* (literally beautiful rice) – is invariably eaten with a meal of meat, curries, seafood and so on, while fried rice and noodles are generally made into a meal on their own, usually for breakfast, a mid-morning snack, lunch or even a late night supper.

This usage accounts for the wide variety of exciting and delicious dishes, based on what may be considered by some to be 'boring' staple foods.

Kway Tiaow Rad Nah Yod Pak

Fried Noodles with Kale & Shrimps

Ingredients

150 gm large shrimps
250 ml chicken stock
150 gm rice noodles
70 gm kale (sliced)
50 gm straw mushrooms (cleaned & halved)
40 gm carrots (peeled & thinly sliced)
1 tsp salted beans (or tinned black beans)
1/2 tbsp oyster sauce
1 tbsp white soya sauce
1 tbsp cornflour
Ground black pepper to taste

Preparation

- Peel & de-vein the shrimps. Set aside.
- Pre-heat a wok, add a little oil & fry the noodles until slightly crispy. Set aside.
- Stir fry the shrimps & vegetables together for 1 minute.
- Pour in chicken stock, adding the oyster sauce, soya sauce & black pepper. Simmer for 3 minutes.
- Mix the cornflour with water until smooth & use to thicken the mixture slightly.
- Pour mixture on top of the noodles & serve.

MEE SAPAM PHAD PAK

Fried 'Sapam' Noodles 'Phuket-Style'

Ingredients

70 gm shrimps
70 gm squid (cleaned & sliced)
70 gm snapper fillet (sliced)
30 gm mussels (steamed out of shell)
150 gm fresh yellow noodles (*sapam*)
70 gm Chinese lettuce or green cabbage (sliced)
20 gm shallot (peeled & sliced)
5-6 cloves garlic (chopped)
1 egg
2 tbsp oyster sauce
1 tbsp black soya sauce

Preparation

- Peel & de-vein the shrimps. Set aside.
- Fry the shallots in a wok until crispy. Set aside.
- Fry the garlic in a hot wok, then add the prepared seafood; stir fry for about 3 minutes until tender.
- Add the sapam noodles & Chinese lettuce; stir fry for a further 2-3 minutes.
- Season with the soya sauce & oyster sauce.
- Break the egg into a serving bowl & pour the noodles on top.
- Toss & serve, garnished with the crispy shallots.

PHAD THAI

Fried Noodles 'Thai-Style'

Ingredients

80 gm large shrimps
120 gm rice noodles
1 egg
50 gm bean sprouts
20 gm salty turnip
50 gm yellow bean curd
20 ml tomato sauce
5 ml chili sauce
Juice of half a lime
Sugar & ground black pepper to taste

For garnish

2 tbsp roasted peanuts (ground)
1/2 lime
20 gm chives
2-3 spring onions

Preparation

- Peel & de-vein the shrimps. Set aside.
- Pre-heat a wok & stir fry the egg; add the noodles, shrimps, bean sprouts, turnip & bean curd.
- Stir fry continuously for about 3 minutes, adding the tomato & chili sauces & lime juice; season with pepper & sugar.
- Serve garnished with the ground peanuts, half the lime, chives & spring onion.

Note

Phad Thai is one of the favourite lunch-time meals throughout the whole of the country. You may hear people comparing one person's *Phad Thai* with another's; a reputation for good *Phad Thai* is a source of great pride to a cook, professional and amateur alike.

KHAO PHAD

FRIED RICE

KHAO OB SAPAROT — PINEAPPLE FRIED RICE

INGREDIENTS

1 pineapple
1 cup steamed rice
7 tsp soya sauce (Maggi)
15 gm carrots (diced small)
15 gm onions (diced small)
20 gm raisins (soaked)
20 gm snowpeas (trimmed)
50 gm chicken breast (cubed)
80 gm white shrimps (peeled & de-veined)
40 gm cashew nuts
1 tsp curry powder

PREPARATION

- Hollow out half a pineapple. Save fruit for the rice.
- Slice half the shrimps, leaving the other half whole.
- Stir fry all ingredients (except whole shrimps) in a hot wok, until meat & shrimps are well cooked.
- Season with soya sauce & place in the pineapple.
- Deep fry the whole shrimps & cashew nuts; place on top for garnish & serve.

KHAO PHAD GOONG — FRIED RICE WITH SHRIMPS

INGREDIENTS

6 pcs white shrimps
1 cup steamed rice
1 egg
50 gm spring onions (sliced)
50 gm tomatoes (chopped)
Black pepper to taste
1 tbsp white soya sauce
50 gm cucumber (sliced)
1 tomato (cut in half)

IN PLACE OF THE SHRIMP, YOU MAY USE ONE OF:

80 gm crab meat – *Poo*
120 gm chicken breast – *Gai*
120 gm pork loin – *Moo*
70 gm squid – *Pla Meuk*

PREPARATION

- Stir fry all the ingredients in a hot wok, until meat is cooked thoroughly. Season with soya sauce.
- Garnish with sliced cucumber & tomato halves.

VEGETABLES

It is ironic that vegetarian food (except during special festivals) is hard to find in Thailand. A visit to one of many early-morning markets will confirm that Thailand has a truly bewildering variety of vegetables, some familiar to visitors and some – such as the infamous *Sataw Bean* – utterly exotic.

Yet few Thais would contemplate a meal based exclusively on vegetables, let alone one without essential ingredients such as fish sauce, oyster sauce, pork fat and so on.

Thais, especially southern Thais, often like to eat vegetables raw with hot chili sauce – a dish called *Nam Prik*. They also – as far as western tastes are concerned – tend to blur the distinction between herbs and vegetables.

However, the majority of vegetables eaten as part of a main meal are stir-fried, a method of cooking that ensures they are crispy, at the same time retaining maximum nutrients.

PHAD PAK RUAM NAAM MAN HOI

STIR-FRIED MIXED VEGETABLES IN OYSTER SAUCE

INGREDIENTS

70 gm snowpeas
100 gm cabbage (large slices)
100 gm Chinese, or regular green, cabbage (large slices)
30 gm straw mushrooms (sliced)
100 gm carrots (peeled & sliced)
70 gm kale (large slices)
50 gm cauliflower (florettes)
2 cloves garlic (crushed)
1 tbsp oyster sauce
2 tbsp white soya sauce
1 tbsp cornflour
Ground black pepper to taste

PREPARATION

- Blanche the cauliflower, carrots, broccoli & mushrooms in boiling water.
- Stir fry the garlic in oil in a hot wok; add the blanched vegetables. Quickly stir fry until hot.
- Season with the pepper, soya sauce & oyster sauce.
- Mix the cornflour with water until smooth & use to thicken the mixture slightly.

OPTIONS

You could use other quick-cooking vegetables in season, such as courgettes or broccoli, for variation.

NOR MAI FARANG PHAD GOONG SOD

Stir-Fried Asparagus with Shrimps

Ingredients

150 gm white shrimps
200 gm asparagus (trimmed)
6-8 cloves garlic (crushed)
1 tbsp oyster sauce
1/4 tsp sesame oil
1 tbsp cornflour
Sugar & ground black pepper to taste

Preparation

- Peel & de-vein the shrimps. Set aside.
- Steam the asparagus. Set aside.
- Heat the sesame oil with a little vegetable in a wok until very hot, then add the garlic & shrimps; stir fry for 1-2 minutes.
- Add the asparagus.
- Add the oyster sauce & seasonings.
- Mix the cornflour with water until smooth & use to thicken the mixture slightly.

Option

If asparagus is not available, you could substitute other fast-cooking, delicate-flavoured vegetables such as snow peas.

KANAA NAAM MAN HOI

SAUTÉED KALE IN OYSTER SAUCE

INGREDIENTS

350 gm kale (peel stems)
2-3 cloves garlic (crushed)
10 gm red chilies (sliced)
1 tbsp oyster sauce
1 tbsp white soya sauce
1 tsp cornflour

PREPARATION

- Heat the oil until very hot in a wok; add the garlic & kale. Stir fry quickly until just tender.
- Add the oyster sauce & soya sauce.
- Mix the cornflour with water until smooth & use to thicken the mixture slightly.

PHAD PAK BOONG FAI DAENG

STIR FRIED MORNING GLORY WITH SALTED BEANS

INGREDIENTS

150 gm Chinese morning glory (washed)
2-3 cloves garlic (crushed)
5 gm red chilies (sliced)
1 tbsp salted black beans
1 tbsp oyster sauce
1 tbsp white soya sauce

PREPARATION

- Stir fry the garlic in a hot wok, then add the morning glory & all other ingredients.

NOTE: The morning glory should be cooked very quickly to keep the vegetable crisp & not over-cooked.

DESSERTS

Thai desserts may, at first, sound strange to the western ear. Certainly a sweet tooth is a requirement for those planning to venture into this part of the Thai menu. However, anyone who has not tasted *Khao Niaow Mamuang* or *Tub Tim Grob* has not experienced the full range of Thai flavours, nor the remarkable extent to which every component of a Thai meal can be balanced, the way every dish has its equal and opposite.

After the richness of a Thai coconut milk curry (*Gaeng Gratik*), the fiery subtleness of a Thai salad and the hot-sour combination of a *Tom Yam*, the cool, delicate offerings of the menu's final chapter will leave your palate refreshed.

Try the few samples included in this section. But remember Thailand's ever-present standby: a loaded platter of exotic fruit.

KHAO NIAOW MAMUANG

Sweet Sticky Rice with Fresh Mango

Ingredients

300 gm sticky rice
1 large can coconut milk
2 pandanus leaves (omit if not available)
100 gm sugar
1 ripe mango (peeled & sliced)
1/3 tsp white sesame seeds
1 pch salt

Preparation

- Wash the sticky rice in several changes of cold water. Soak for 24 hours.
- Steam the rice (ideally in a bamboo steamer) for about 20 minutes. The rice should be gluey in texture.
- Gently simmer the coconut milk, sugar & salt with the pandanus leaves until they form a thick sweet sauce.
- Pour the coconut sauce over the hot steamed rice & stir. Cover and stand for 30 minutes (until the rice has absorbed all the sauce).
- Serve the rice at room temperature with the sliced mango & sesame seeds on top.

TUB TIM GROB

Jellied Water Chestnuts in Syrup with Crushed Ice

Ingredients

20 water chestnuts in syrup
6 drops red food colouring
100 gm tapioca flour
160 gm sugar
1 cup (250ml) coconut milk
2 pandanus leaves (omit if not available)
1 pch salt
Crushed ice

Preparation

- Cut the water chestnuts into quarters.
- Mix the food colouring with 2 tbsp water, add the water chestnuts; remove from the liquid when they are coloured red.
- Coat the water chestnuts in tapioca flour.
- Place in water & bring to the boil. Cook until the flour has clarified, then drain off the water; set aside.
- Place pandanus leaves & sugar in 1 cup of water; boil until all the sugar is dissolved to make a syrup.
- Simmer the coconut milk to reduce by 1/4 in volume; add the salt.
- Serve the water chestnuts in the syrup & reduced coconut milk, on a little crushed ice.

BUA LOY KHAI WAAN

COCONUT DUMPLINGS WITH QUAIL EGGS

INGREDIENTS

200 gm sticky rice flour
4 cups (1 litre) coconut milk
100 gm water for dough
4 quail eggs
20 gm fresh ginger (grated)
200 gm palm sugar (or soft brown sugar)
1 pandanus leaf (omit if not available)
1 pch salt

PREPARATION

- Mix the sticky rice flour with the water & knead into a dough.
- Mould into ball shapes about 1 cm in diameter to form dumplings.
- Place the dumplings in boiling water; remove when they float to the top.
- Boil the coconut milk with the palm sugar, salt, ginger & pandanus leaf for 7 minutes.
- Add the dumplings to the coconut milk mixture.
- Add the quail eggs & boil for another 30 seconds. Serve immediately.

KHANOM KROK

Coconut Pudding with Chives

Ingredients

480 gm wheat flour
400 gm steamed rice
400 ml water
1 large can coconut milk
80 gm chives (finely chopped)
1 tsp salt
1 tsp sugar

Preparation

- Mix wheat flour with 300 ml water & leave to stand for 10 minutes.
- Mix the steamed rice with 100 ml water, add to the flour/water mixture, then add the coconut milk to form a batter.
- Heat a lightly oiled Thai pudding pan until medium hot.
- Pour the batter into the pan, filling the holes 3/4 full.
- Sprinkle with chives & cover.
- Cook for about 2-3 minutes
- Remove the puddings with a spoon & serve warm or at room temperature.

Helpful hint

In place of a Thai pudding pan, use a regular baking tray suitable for small muffins or cup cakes.

A
B
C
D
E
F

COCKTAILS

ALCOHOLIC

Blue Lagoon (B)

1 oz vodka
1 oz Blue Curaçao
1 oz lemon juice
1/2 oz sugar syrup
2 oz Sprite

Mix all ingredients in a shaker with ice. Shake well & pour into a highball glass. Top up with Sprite. Decorate with a slice of lemon.

Kahlua Hommer (C)

1 oz Kahlua
1/2 oz Barcardi Rum
1/2 oz Bailey's Irish Cream
2 scoops vanilla ice cream

Blend all ingredients with crushed ice & serve in highball glass; decorate with strawberry.

Bangtao Sunset (F)

1/2 oz Barcardi Rum
1/2 oz crème de coconut
1/2 oz crème de banana
2 oz pineapple juice
1 oz orange juice
1/2 oz grenadine syrup

Blend all ingredients with crushed ice & serve in a whole pineapple.

NON-ALCOHOLIC

Coco Colada (A)

30 oz coconut juice or coconut milk
3 oz pineapple juice
1 scoop coconut ice cream
1 oz sugar syrup
1/2 oz grenadine syrup

Blend all ingredients together with crushed ice & serve in a fresh young coconut.

Re-Charger (D)

2 oz pineapple juice
2 oz orange juice
1 banana
2 tsp plain yoghurt
1 tsp honey

Blend all ingredients together with crushed ice & serve in a tall glass. Decorate with a slice of orange & banana.

Laguna Royal (E)

3 oz grapefruit juice
4 oz orange juice
1/2 oz lemon juice
1 oz sugar syrup
1 oz soda water

Blend all ingredients together with crushed ice & serve in a tall glass; add the soda water. Decorate with a slice of orange.

Chef Theerati's Tips

Gai Hor Bai Toey (Page 31)

Follow these directions to make the pandanus leaf parcel.

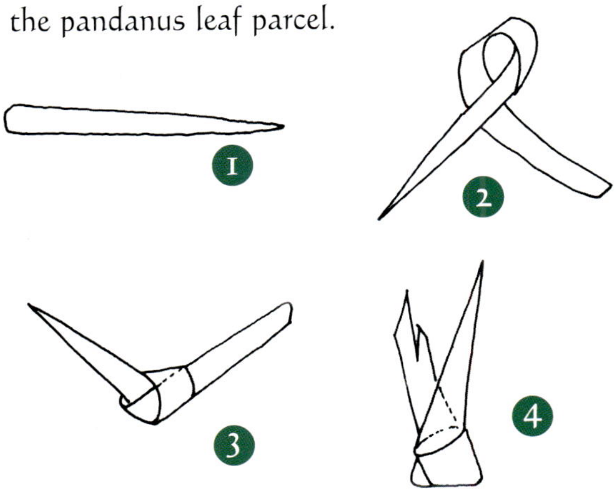

Butterfly Prawns

To 'butterfly cut' prawns, lay the prawn flat on its side & bring your knife blade along the back, cutting only half-way. Then open & apply light pressure to the 'butterfly'.

Prik Naam Pla

Prik Naam Pla (spicy fish sauce) is served with most rice dishes in Thailand. It comprises finely chopped small chilies soaked in fish sauce. It is served as a condiment and is a great way – for those who like it hot – to 'spice up' most dishes.

Be aware, though, that the other purpose of *Prik Naam Pla* is to add saltiness to a dish. Be careful how much you use.

Hot Oil

Soak dry chilies in oil & keep it on hand for cooking if you like a more spicy flavour.

Mushrooms

Where straw mushrooms are called for, they produce the best result – but you may replace with any mushrooms if straw mushrooms are not available.

Garnish

For a unique garnish for many dishes, take a cucumber, cut grooves in the skin along the length, and slice at an angle.

Garlic

Where chopped garlic is recommended, you can use ready-minced garlic for speed.

Coconut Milk

Coconut milk is susceptible to curdling. Once you have added coconut milk to a dish, avoid bringing the liquid to the boil.

Try Them Raw

Serve raw vegetables as an accompaniment to lunch or dinner. Popular choices include carrots, celery & cucumber. It's a great way of cooling & clearing the palate.

Freshly Squeezed

Freshly squeezed juices, lemon & soda water or iced tea are popular drinks that Thais enjoy with their food.

Experiment!

We have suggested alternatives for the main component of many meat & seafood dishes. Once you are familiar with the taste combinations, experiment by changing the main component. Variation is the essence of Thai cooking.